The Complete Shorter Piano Works of Charles E. Ives (1874–1954)
James B. Sinclair, Executive Editor
Donald Berman, General Editor

Volume 3: Miscellaneous Works
Edited by James B. Sinclair and Thomas M. Brodhead

TABLE OF CONTENTS

Volume 3 of *The Complete Shorter Piano Works of Charles Ives* is a compilation of miscellaneous works by Ives. These works range from small-scale early pieces to larger scale settings of music related to the *"Concord" Sonata*. The volume also contains critical performance editions of four important genre pieces by Ives: *Varied Air and Variations, Waltz-Rondo, Three-Page Sonata*, and *Set of Five Take-Offs*. Finally, the compendium includes the first publication of Ives's original piano version of *The "St. Gaudens"* ("Black March"), more known in its orchestrated version as "The 'St. Gaudens' in Boston Common" from *Orchestral Set No. 1: Three Places in New England*.

Two major works within this volume have a unique and complicated history. Thomas M. Brodhead's prefaces to *The Celestial Railroad* and *Four Transcriptions from "Emerson"* (below) delineate those works' gestation, re-working, and final editing.

AMP 8321
First Printing: September 2022

ISBN: 978-1-70517-017-5

Associated Music Publishers, Inc.

DISTRIBUTED BY

www.halleonard.com
www.wisemusicclassical.com

D1454057

Minuetto, Op. 4, S. 119
[Invention in D], S. 118

The earliest work in this volume is Ives's *Minuetto, Op. 4*. Ives was twelve when he composed it. He studiously supplied opus numbers to his earliest works. (He would abandon the chronology system by the time he was in college.) On album leaves that contained canonic exercises, Ives penciled this first complete surviving piece for piano. (One of the fragments on verso is "New Year's Dance – 1886", included in the Appendix.) His father, George Edward Ives, copied the *Minuetto* in ink. Even within the simple conceit of a classical minuet, Ives shows a penchant for tantalizing the music with truncated phrasing. Indeed, George considered regularizing the opening six-measure phrase by making it eight measures long. He then thought better of his heavy edit, crossed it out, flipped the page upside down, and re-copied young Charlie's work as originally composed.

The impetus for *[Invention in D]* Allegretto could have been an assignment by Ives's Yale composition teacher Horatio Parker to write a piece in the style of a Bach *Invention*. (Ives's *Organ Fugue in E♭* has been confirmed by musicologist Gayle Magee as a result of a Parker assignment at Yale.) To that end, the work's rhythmic identity of a dotted quarter tied into a measure of running sixteenth notes resembles Bach's *Sinfonia XIII* in A minor, BWV 799. For this reason, John Kirkpatrick designated the piece as "Invention in D." Ives's manuscript is untitled; it is simply marked "Allegretto." Within the ternary form of the work are touches of barbershop quartet harmonies, and a homespun melody that brings the Baroque example down to earth as Ives knew it.

The Genre Works

[Set of Five Take-Offs], S. 122
Three-Page Sonata, S. 89
Waltz-Rondo, S. 125
Varied Air and Variations, S. 124

A bound volume that includes piano pieces (known as "Songbook B" because it contains songs as well as other compositions) was handed to John Kirkpatrick in 1938. Within the book are five character pieces bearing titles and the roman numerals i – v supplied by Ives. The five pieces were contiguous, taking up three consecutive pages. This suggests that they were intended as a set. The editorial title "Set of Five Take-Offs" was supplied by John Kirkpatrick, adopted from hints in Ives's *Memos* (published in 1972, compiled and edited by Kirkpatrick). In *Memos*, Ives refers to "some piano pieces…take-offs, etc. [that have] wide jumps in the counterpoint and lines.)" Though Ives's note specifically mentions piano works, his only direct listing of "Take-Offs" are in his various "Lists," one of which reads: "Cartoons or Take-Offs (academic, athletic, anthropolitic, economic, tragic) for large and small orchestras."

In "The Seen and Unseen (or Sweet and Tough)," Ives casts a generically old-fashioned tune in C major against dissonant harmonizations. That polarity is enhanced with dynamic markings that indicate a foreground singing line (the "Seen") against distant-sounding chords (the "Unseen"). In the movement's final measures, Ives writes a polytonal two-handed chord that dissolves, in the manner of a Schumannesque gradual lifting of notes, to a C major close.

"Rough and Ready" or "The Jumping Frog" is a take-off on the Mark Twain story, "The Celebrated Jumping Frog of Calaveras County." (Mark Twain was a close friend of Ives's father-in-law Reverend Joseph Twitchell.) It is an etude-like movement of perpetual motion and polyrhythmic counterpoint. Within the moving right-hand quintuplets are two-note dyad accents played by the thumb. Ives's marginalia notes that "The thumb is the frog." The music tumbles forward and culminates heroically, at the Presto, with tunes from the finale to Ives's *First Symphony* (1898) and a college football song.

"Song without (good) Words" is a spoof of the Mendelssohns's lyrical *Songs Without Words (Lied ohne Worte)*. Ives opens with an introductory F major lilting accompaniment, under a repeated minor 9th in the right hand. When the melody begins, Ives reveals that the minor 9th is a transposition of what would have been a typical minor second passing tone in an otherwise unremarkable tune. The shift gives the melody a surprising and humorous contour. He follows with heavily voiced appogiaturas (m. 7) and leading tones transposed to a descending major seventh (mm. 10–11). The melodic narrative becomes more richly harmonized in mm. 15–23. Though begun as caricature of a romantic genre, the piece develops with pungent harmonies and emotive impact. The harmonically unresolved ending is mysterious, and is also an upbeat to the opening of the fourth movement.

"Scene Episode" is a paraphrase from the last movement of the *Sonata No. 1 for Piano* (1909–1922). The hymntune HAPPY DAY lifts out of a ruminative procession of widely spaced chords in the right hand, accompanied by broadly arpeggiated chords in the left. It ends with an F/F♯ chord over a C major bass. This acts as a kind of plagal cadence to the fifth movement.

The pithy "Bad Resolutions and Good WAN!" juxtaposes sugary sweet suspensions ("bad resolutions") with a penultimate measure of no-holds-barred dissonance ("good one"). It was composed on New Year's Eve, 1907, as Ives was about to embark on the start of his own insurance firm, co-founded with Julian Myrick. Though clamorously funny, the resounding ending is powerfully definitive.

The *Three-Page Sonata* was first drafted during a vacation at Saranac Lake, NY, that Ives spent with Yale friend David Twitchell and his family, including Ives's eventual wife, Harmony Twitchell. That pencil score is the sole source for this edition. The work, so titled because it was sketched on three pages, is an early foray into (quasi) sonata form.

The "first movement" plays with sonata-allegro form. It contains an exposition and development. However, the anticipated recapitulation is replaced by the entirely new music of the second movement, radically shifting the focus. "Movement 1" opens with a phrase that starts with a declamation in 4ths of the B-A-C-H motif. (Ives would later employ this motive frequently as an inner voice, including in *"Concord" Sonata*, p. 12, system 2, m. 1.) Within the "first movement" chordal build-up are bugle calls (m. 1, b. 18) and quotes of "My Country 'tis of thee" (m.1, b. 31). The quiet "second movement" opens in 4/4, with a left-hand G-major arpeggio repeated in a 5/8 pattern. The piece carries forth the Bach-like motives of movement one and gradually leads to variations on, and statement of, "Westminster Chimes" (which also appears in *"Concord" Sonata*, p. 55, system 2, b. 9 middle voice). Ives remarks in the marginalia (mm. 16–21): "better to have another player or bells or celesta top."

The "finale" is stamped by Ives's favored genre of his early works: the march (see preface to *The Complete Shorter Piano Works of Charles E. Ives*, Vol. 1). The introduction is a row of eleven notes that, just after ending in an F-B tritone vamp, culminates in the missing twelfth note of the row, C. The ensuing C major March quickly slides into LH vamps in the keys C♯ and E (those key areas follow the same first two notes of the opening row). The march, and its development through notes of the opening row, is interrupted by snippets of rag-time, waltz, and other triumphant crashes. It ends in C major with a rattling quasi-plagal cadence.

Waltz-Rondo is a rondo in waltz tempo, in two alternating keys: D major and D♭ major. In the rondo refrain, the LH rather conventionally arpeggiates through the tonic and dominant of D major, while the RH alternates measures in D and D♭ major. Ives was intent in pointing out these bi-tonalities, and his score indicates the alternate key signatures bar by bar (as in this edition.) This quick key signature alternation gives the theme an ingeniously slippery humor. The opening introduction, before the theme, is primarily a pedal on A major, with the RH wending its way sequentially upward in two-note slurs from A♭ to the tonic D major.

The rondo consists of six episodes, set between restatements of the refrain. Episode 1 (rehearsal letter A), is a melodic variation of the refrain, beginning with an inversion of the refrain's characteristic starting notes F♯ and G. Episode 2 (letter B) is the first of etude-like chromatic and polyrhythmic excursions. The left hand sequences pairs of tritones, but with a phrasing of the three-beat waltz pattern holding firm. The right hand is in groups of 10 eighth notes, sequencing around the circle of 5ths. The pace picks up when the left hand pattern goes into cut time, until it reaches the calm of episode 3 (letter C). This quiet interlude maintains an A^7 arpeggiation in 3/4, with the right hand in a B♭ minor/D♭ variation on the fourth measure of the rondo refrain.

Each episode from here to the end increases in activity and virtuosic demand. Episode 4 (letter D) resembles Ives's *Study No. 7* for piano (see *The Complete Shorter Piano Works of Charles E. Ives*, Vol. 2), where he sets a strong chordal bass progression of I-IV-V (D-G-A) on each bar's downbeat; the 2nd and 3rd beats are voiced by the other nine notes of the 12-note chromatic scale, with the middle staffs as a block chord, and the top part in quick roulades of 4-, 3-, and 2-note phrases. Episode 5 (letter E), essentially a variation on episode 2, contains left-hand chromatic movement in leaping octaves with the right-hand in quickly moving broken chords. Ives leads one to think that the simpler waltz-rondo refrain returns halfway through the episode (m. 64), before the variation continues, sped up in a stretto-like alternation between the hands. At episode 6 (letter F), Ives reaches an apex of activity. The left hand pits a pedal point D against an off-beat setting of his favored triumphant tune "Columbia, the Gem of The Ocean." In the right hand, Ives keeps the accents and rhythmic compressions going, all the while quoting snippets of the fiddle tunes "Fisher's Hornpipe" (m. 75), "Turkey in the Straw" (m. 79), "Sailor's Hornpipe" (m. 85), and "The White Cockade" (m. 87).

The Coda is a recap of all that has occurred up to that point. Each episode is represented in a quick succession of, on average, four bars per episode, culminating in a varied reprise of episode 4. Ives was well aware of the technical demands of the piece, and in the manuscript he sketched out the outline of a "Nicer Coda" (see further at: charlesives.org for the diplomatic transcription of the manuscript).

Varied Air and Variations is a short rigorous set of variations on an atonal row of eleven notes (the missing twelfth note, B♭, underpins the harmony in the intervening refrains). Each variation repeats the theme verbatim, however, the speed, registral shifts, and accompanying material all make for radical shifts in character.

In the sketches Ives described the theme as "The old stone wall aroun[d] the orchard, none of these stones eggsactly the same size" ("eggsactly" is a tmetic pun on stone eggs + exactly; the title of the piece is also a tmetic pun, as it could be heard as "Very Darin' Variations"). Ives voices the theme for two hands in unison, three octaves apart. For the organist Ives, this voicing is known as trisdiapson. The row is built primarily on perfect 4ths and 2nds. The sense of note diversity is enhanced by varied rhythmic values. (In the manuscript, the idea of "stone eggs" as equated to note value is actualized by Ives's varied sizes of written noteheads).

In the sketches Ives described the first variation as "The Stone wall (ink line) *ffffff* and the other notes *pppppppp* = things & sounds in the distance…", combines the soft introductory and interluding chorales (or "protests" [about the atonal theme], as he slyly called them) with the theme exchanged between the high and low registers.

Variations 2 and 3 are in march time, and repeat the theme twice (the repeat starts in mm. 41 and 69 on the 3rd sixteenth). Variation 2 is an exercise in two-hand inversion. Variation 3 is a canon, beginning a 5th apart.

Variation 4, the Adagio, sets the theme once-unrepeated, augmented, slowed, and harmonized as in a Bach chorale (the B-A-C-H theme appears in the left hand at the start of m. 78). The ensuing C major fanfare interlude has been prepared for a while by the theme's anchor on the note B (leading tone of C), and the previous interlude's top voice-leading (A♭-B♭- ?). Described cheekily by Ives as "applause" (for its tonality after atonality), the C major chords can equally be heard as a triumphant arrival. (This is the case in other Ives pieces included in this volume: *The St. Gaudens*, m. 61; *Set of Five Take-Offs*: "Bad Resolutions and Good WAN!", m. 10; *Three-Page Sonata*, m. 106.) The coda stitches together reprises of mm. 38–39, 25a–33a, and mm. 41–43, played "faster than ever" and loudly. Hardly recognizable as a repeat of "things and sounds in the distance," the coda ends in dodecophonic glory.

The "St. Gaudens" ("Black March"), S. 683i

The eventual first movement of the orchestral masterpiece *Three Places in New England* began as a piano work called simply "The St Gaudens." The piece, written in ink, remained in that state from 1910 to 1915, when Ives fleshed out the piano score and then began to add pencil emendations toward the orchestral work. Meanwhile, Ives played the piece and referred to it as "my Black March." In *Memos* (p. 51), Ives recalled having the piece with him when he showed Walter Damrosch his *First Symphony* in 1910. He also recalled, "I also played this Black March (almost in the shape that it's in today)…this was either in the fall of 1910 or 1911…" (p. 87). On the manuscript are notes for potentially using the piece as a culminating movement to a piano sonata (never realized). On the opening page he wrote:

> III. 1. The Common (Largo) (Emerson & Park Ch[urch]) 2. The
> Abolishionists (allegro) Wendell Phillips – Faneuil Hall 3. "The St. Gaudens"
> (Adagio-Andante) "moving marching faces of souls."

Augustus Saint-Gaudens (1848–1907) was the American sculptor who designed the Adams Memorial, the Peter Cooper, and John A. Logan monuments. His masterpiece was the bas-relief in the Boston Common (still standing across from the State House on Beacon Street), commemorating Colonel Robert Gould Shaw and his "Black regiment," who fought for the Union in the American Civil War. Described as Saint-Gaudens's "symphony in bronze," it took fourteen years to complete (1883–1897).

Ives's slow march begins with octave bass repetitions on the notes A and C. These are the second and third notes to Stephen Foster's "Old Black Joe," which starts with the words "I'm coming, I'm coming, for my head is hanging low." (The A-C ostinato would figure again as the first two of the three-note ostinato in "Thoreau" from *"Concord" Sonata*; Thoreau was a vocal abolitionist.) Other snippets from the tune appear throughout the piece, as part of the melodic thread, and within modulating harmonies. Other quotes embedded in the unfolding string of phrases include "The Battle Cry of Freedom" (beat 50), "Marching Through Georgia" (beat 141), and "Massa's in de Cold Ground" (beat 240).

Rhythmically, the slow moving bass repetitions depict the trudging of the regiment soldiers. As the tempo picks up, Ives wrote in the margins:

> whatever holding back & variation in tempo let it be but little & not a marked
> contrast. When a mass of men march up a hill there is an unconscious
> slowing up the drum seems to follow the feet rather than feet the drum in
> case as on level ground.

As compared to the more elaborate orchestral version, the piano version's percussiveness brings the persistent "slow march" to the fore. On keyboard, one hears the clipped inflections of marchers, and chord voicings that anticipate the blues.

Donald Berman

The Celestial Railroad, S. 116
Four Transcriptions from "Emerson", S. 123

The Celestial Railroad

The history of Ives's *The Celestial Railroad* is intertwined with the development of the "Comedy" movement of his *Fourth Symphony*. The origin of both pieces can be traced to the first decade of the twentieth century, when Ives began composing a group of overtures and concertos in tribute to Transcendentalist authors. He dubbed the prospective series "Men of Literature," and he intended to compose (among other works) an *Emerson Overture*, a *Hawthorne Piano Concerto*, and an *Orchard House Overture* (named for the New England home of the Alcotts).

In the early 1910s, Ives abandoned this orchestral project, but not without finding new uses for the musical materials he had created thus far. Between approximately 1912 and 1915, he reworked the "Men of Literature" pieces mentioned above as the first three movements of his *Sonata No. 2 for Piano ("Concord, Mass., 1840–60")*, the *"Concord" Sonata*. He simplified many of the passages as he reworked the materials, perhaps fearing that the harmonic and contrapuntal novelty of the music would be too complex for the public of the day (a tendency seen in much of Ives's compositional efforts of the 1910s, when his hopes of a public performance were at least slightly elevated, if not high). But at the same time that the *"Concord" Sonata* was taking shape, Ives composed his *Fourth Symphony* (an uncompromising composition, by comparison) and he apparently put the *Hawthorne Piano Concerto* into it as the "Comedy" movement.

In 1919, Ives engaged New York publisher G. Schirmer to engrave and print the *"Concord" Sonata* for his own private distribution (i.e., not for public sale), and the handsome hardbound copies were delivered to him in January 1921. However, upon seeing his music on the printed page Ives became dissatisfied with the compromises he had made in recasting the *Sonata*'s musical materials. Ever the imaginative and creative reviser, Ives solved his quandary by creating two new works: In one case, the goal was to restore lost complexity; in the other, the goal was to generate new materials as well as amplify existing ones.

In the first case, he selected four passages from the "Emerson" movement of the *"Concord" Sonata* and restored to them the harmonic complexity of the *Emerson Overture*—the orchestral parent to "Emerson." Specifically, he restored dissonances that had been abandoned while deriving the Sonata movement from its orchestral predecessor. He also added to those passages certain sections from the *Overture* that had been omitted in the *Sonata*. These passages were grouped together and became the piano solo *Four Transcriptions from "Emerson."* (Harmonic revisions to the *Sonata* materials in the Transcriptions—but not the additional sections from the *Overture*—were later incorporated into the *"Concord" Sonata*'s 1947 second edition.)

As a companion piece to *Four Transcriptions from "Emerson,"* and in an apparent effort to create a "Concord Suite," Ives crafted a transcription of the "Hawthorne" movement of the *Sonata* that would specifically follow the plot line of Hawthorne's short story, "The Celestial Rail-road," a parody of John Bunyan's well-known "The Pilgrim's Progress." (The transcription therefore contrasts with its parental *Sonata* movement, which is a kaleidoscopic depiction of unrelated story elements taken from many of Hawthorne's different narrative writings.) This new tone-poem for piano, which Ives unambiguously titled *The Celestial Railroad*, was first assembled no earlier than 1921 and likely no later than 1923. Presumably, as with the *Emerson Transcriptions*, *The Celestial Railroad* restored some passages of the *Sonata*'s "Hawthorne" movement to the shape they had assumed in the *Hawthorne Piano Concerto*.

Ives evidently saw *The Celestial Railroad* as an improvement on its sources: he presumably removed the *Hawthorne Piano Concerto* from the *Fourth Symphony* (the lack of a surviving manuscript makes this a point for debate), orchestrated *The Celestial Railroad*, and added the resulting orchestral tone-poem to the *Fourth Symphony* as its "Comedy" movement, the wildest and most outrageous orchestral composition in his entire symphonic output.

The earliest documented public performance of *The Celestial Railroad* was given by Anton Rovinsky on 30 October 1928 at the Albany Institute of History and Art in Albany, New York. Rovinsky played the work frequently thereafter, and he was apparently the work's sole performer during Ives's lifetime. The last documented performance by Rovinsky of this piece was the one he gave over New York radio station WNYC on 22 February 1951 as part of its American Music Festival, coincidentally the same day Ives's *Second Symphony* was premiered at Carnegie Hall by Leonard Bernstein and the New York Philharmonic.

The first public performance of the present edition of *The Celestial Railroad* was given by Alan Mandel on 21 March 1996 on a concert for the Sonneck Society for American Music at the American University in Washington, D.C.

The Program of the Work

The Celestial Railroad (titled "Phantasy" on one manuscript) is a tone-poem on "The Celestial Rail-road" by Nathaniel Hawthorne, in this case a scene-by-scene musical depiction of the short story. In Hawthorne's tale (itself, as mentioned above, a trope on Bunyan's "The Pilgrim's Progress"), a nameless narrator falls asleep and dreams of a fantastic train that speeds its passengers in nineteenth-century comfort to the Celestial City. (This modern convenience is eschewed by the character Christian and his fellow pilgrim travelers who take a difficult foot path to the metropolis of all heavenly rewards, thereby providing a constant counterpoint to the narrator's comparatively cushy journey.) Befriended by a Mr. Smooth-it-away, the narrator boards the train—filled with passengers with equally damning hyphenated names: Mr. Live-for-the-world, Mr. Hide-sin-the-heart, etc.— just before it springs into motion. The train passes many horrible sights, makes stops at temptation-filled towns such as Vanity Fair (where the passengers indulge in high-society pleasantries), and finally comes to rest at Beulah Land on the river Jordan. Everyone leaves the train to take a ferry across the river to the Celestial City. Once the boat is in motion, however, the narrator discovers that his companion Mr. Smooth-it-away is no longer with him but is back on shore, reverting to his true demonic form. The narrator realizes that all has been a hoax and tries to jump from the boat, but a splash of deathly cold water from one of the boat's wheels shocks him awake, and there the comic nightmare ends.

Ives's piano fantasy follows Hawthorne's tale in this manner: The dream begins (mm. 1–21); the train warms up and takes off with whistle blasts (mm. 22–48); various horrible sights are passed (mm. 49–97); a high society social is celebrated at Vanity Fair (mm. 98–103); more miles whiz by on the train (mm. 103–147); an initial glimpse of Beulah Land is had by the passengers (mm. 148–150); one "last and horrible" scream is made by the locomotive engine (mm. 151–158); Beulah Land is reached (mm. 159–168); the ferry is boarded and the dream ends (mm. 169–175); the narrator awakes to the sound of Fourth of July celebrations at Concord (mm. 176–209: not part of Hawthorne's story, but made explicit in Henry Bellamann's program note to the premiere of the *Fourth Symphony*'s "Comedy" movement in 1927, most of which note is clearly ghost-written by Ives himself.)

Four Transcriptions from "Emerson"

Ives's *Four Transcriptions from "Emerson"* is a transitional work that bridges the 1921 and 1947 printed versions of the "Emerson" movement of his *"Concord" Sonata*. The *Sonata*'s gestation began during the first decade of the century, when Ives first began work on a series of overtures to pay tribute to Transcendentalist authors. The prospective works included an *Emerson Overture*, a *Hawthorne Piano Concerto*, and an *Orchard House Overture* (the title referring to the New England home of the Alcotts).

Around 1910 Ives became dissatisfied with the project: He still wished to honor his beloved authors with original music, but his chosen orchestral genre no longer seemed appropriate. Ives evidently solved the problem by recasting the materials from the above-named works as the first three movements of a massive piano sonata. This new work crystallized between 1912 and 1915, and in 1919 Ives engaged New York music publisher G. Schirmer to have it printed privately (i.e., for his own personal distribution). The engraving of the *Sonata* was formidable and time-consuming for the Schirmer staff, but in January 1921 he received the red buckram-bound printings of his keyboard masterpiece in what was to become its first edition (bearing a subtly different wording in its title than found in its subsequent publications), *Second Pianoforte Sonata, "Concord, Mass., 1840–60".*

However, in recasting the overtures for piano, Ives had eliminated some of the harmonic complexity of the music. The reasons he did this are unclear, but the musical tastes of the American public were very conservative at the time, and perhaps Ives was attempting to prevent or reduce a negative critical reaction to his work. He also bypassed certain substantial sections of the *Emerson Overture* when adopting its music for the "Emerson" movement in the Sonata; the music in that movement was therefore never correlative with its parent in a measure-by-measure manner, and was crafted that way by deliberate design whose reasoning we may now only speculate.

After receiving the printings, Ives apparently began to regret simplifying and omitting materials from the *Emerson Overture* in the "Emerson" *Sonata* movement. To remedy his compromises, Ives crafted *Four Transcriptions from "Emerson"*, a piano transcription of four sections from the *Emerson Overture*, the first section heavily laden with Overture sectional restorations. (His esteem for the result is manifest in the fact that he employed his finest copyist, Emil Hanke, to make the final hand copy.) He also apparently reconciled his *Hawthorne Concerto* with the "Hawthorne" *Sonata* movement, reworking it extensively, donning the result "The Celestial Railroad," and later orchestrating it to become the extraordinary "Comedy" movement of *Symphony No. 4*. Unlike the scenario with the Emerson music, however, in which manuscripts to the *Emerson Overture* survive, a lack of any surviving *Hawthorne Concerto* manuscript material makes its reconciliation with the "Hawthorne" of the *Sonata* not only speculative but a subject for debate. That notwithstanding, the development of the "Comedy" movement—including its premiere in 1927 and its publication in Henry Cowell's *New Music* quarterly in 1929—and other final polishing work on *Symphony No. 4* left little time for the Emerson music, which Ives then took up again in the 1930s.

First by means of private electronic recording for aural review, and then through a written reworking of the materials—both on copies of the *Concord* printings as well as on positive photostats of the *Transcriptions*—Ives reshaped the Emerson materials in the *Sonata* throughout the 1930s and into the 1940s, restoring their original harmonic complexity as found in the surviving *Emerson Overture* manuscripts. The result was the second and final edition of *Concord*, first published in 1947 by Arrow Music Press and then by Associated Music Publishers in 1957 with its defining title, *Piano Sonata No. 2, "Concord Mass., 1840–1860"*, the version employed most often by pianists to this day. Arguably, the most substantial differences between the first edition and the second edition are found in the "Emerson" movement (even though all movements received fresh edits by Ives), and almost all of the changes to the "Emerson" movement were worked out in the compositional evolution of the *Transcriptions*.

Correlation with the "Emerson" Movement

As the *Transcriptions* correlate with "Emerson" in the second, 1947 edition of *Concord*, the correlation between the two works is summarized in this chart for reference:

Transcription	"Emerson" movement from *Concord*, 2nd edition
I	Page 1 through page 2, line 1. However, mm. 2–12 (in this edition) correspond to a passage in the *Emerson Overture* that is not duplicated in the *Sonata*'s "Emerson."
II	Page 6, line 1 through all of page 11.
III	Page 14, line 3, measure 3 through page 16, line 4.
IV	Page 17, line 4 through all of page 19.

An early and surprising dating of the *Transcriptions* is provided in a letter from Ives to John Kirkpatrick on 11 November 1935: Transcription number one was created between 1915 and 1918, and the remaining transcriptions were created between 1922 and 1923. However, patches from the 1921 private printing of the entire *"Concord"* *Sonata* are found throughout all of the manuscript sources that—importantly—are not merely sketches to the *Transcriptions*. The presence of these patches would seem to contradict this early dating of the first Transcription. Furthermore, sketches outlining all four Transcriptions in a copy of the 1921 *Concord* (source Kr in the Critical Commentary)—sketches that seem to predate the work by copyists Reis and Hanke—would contradict Ives's claim to Kirkpatrick. The manuscript sources would therefore suggest that work on the composition took place after 1921, following the chronology established in the opening section of this Preface.

Publicization, Performance, and Recording

Ives thought highly of the *Transcriptions*, for he submitted them to the magazine *Musicalia* of Havanna, Cuba in 1929. In addition to this submission, Ives evidently gave copies of the work to musicians for performance. For example, the English pianist Arthur Hardcastle played the second transcription as early as 19 September 1928. Also, John Kirkpatrick has concluded that the third Transcription, Largo, was performed by Oscar Ziegler on a program given at the New School on 6 January 1931. In his *Memos* of 1932, Ives wrote about the *Transcriptions*:

> Some of the four transcriptions as I play them today, especially the first and third, are changed considerably. I think I shall make a record, perhaps playing each movement two or three different ways. This will be done for my own satisfaction and study, and also to save the trouble and eyesight of copying it all out. After the record is made, Mr. Henry Cowell, Mr. Nicolas Slonimsky, or some other acoustical genius, could write it down for me—and probably better than I can.

And so he did. Between 1933 and 1943, on four different occasions and in as many different locales, Ives recorded himself performing excerpts from the *Transcriptions* along with other original works in a style that vacillated between manuscript-accuracy and improvisation. These were issued in full on the 1999 Composers Recordings' album, "Ives Plays Ives" (CD 810, later transfered to New World Records 80642-2). Of note are the renditions of the *Transcriptions*, which greatly outnumber the other music recorded and bespeak of Ives's preoccupation with the material during the last quarter of his life.

Editorial Focus

This edition is based primarily on the clear copy made by Emil Hanke, circa 1925. Ives's original manuscript score and the copy made by Reis were consulted for clarification of detail. Other sources were consulted as indicated in the Critical Commentary on the Charles Ives Society website.

In order to serve the performer, Ives's densely contrapuntal writing—originally leaping from one staff to the next without consideration for clear hand division, and often written on three staves—has been clarified so that each hand keeps to its own staff and so that the apprehension of independent voices is transparent. Dashed barlines in the second Transcription, mm. 9–13 are original to Ives (manifestly an attempt to clarify phrasing), but the dashed barline at m. 16 in that Transcription is editorial, and is distinguished from Ives's by extending only through the white space between the staves (i.e., not extending into the staves).

One passage in which Ives's idiosyncratic notation has been preserved, however, is in the second Transcription, mm. 9–13, 19–23, 27–32. That section contains notes that employ greater rhythmic durations than what is obviously intended, most famously the series of whole-note chords in the right hand that are to be played in the time of quarter notes in mm. 19–23. It may seem that these chords are written with augmented time values for emphasis, but Ives's writings clarify his actual intentions:

> Through here the r.h. whole notes playing on the quarter notes (beats) are used instead of (black) nice quarter notes to suggest to the eye what the ear hears—the tones held with each other as the sound diminishes quickly when the next blow comes along. In the concerto score from here through the second brace, P. 10 [of the printed "Emerson" movement], violins and violas were divided into groups of four players—assuming that the upper string orchestra has thirty-two players—each group taking their chord line and all players holding their own notes until the end of the measure, though diminishing considerably before the next group plays their part of the verse.

Regarding the other graphically augmented notes in this Transcription, Ives continues:

> (In other passages, the notes are held and decreasing, but not quite to the same extent as in this passage.) The sustaining pedal (here) will sometimes (give) have a nearer impression to what is wanted than perhaps the 32 strings would always do.

Therefore, we know from these memos that the chords in mm. 19–23 are written to convey their original orchestration and sonic effect in the seminal *Emerson Overture*. The other visually augmented notes are apparently intended to be sustained in similar fashion, an interpretation evinced by their original durations in the *Overture*. These notations have been retained both for musicological integrity as well as for an expansion of the performer's possible interpretation of the sections in question.

The Hanke Positives

Of special note to the analyst are the five sets of positive photostats of the Hanke copy (henceforth the "Hanke positives"). These were apparently used by Ives for experimental revisions to the music in the 1930s or 1940s (exact date unknown, but most likely after he had begun making sound recordings of the *Transcriptions*). The changes that Ives made on the Hanke positives are wildly inconsistent, and the revisions are written one on top of another in an almost unreadable thorn bush of conflicting ideas. To illustrate the extremely complex and at the same time endlessly fascinating nature of the Hanke positives, a "clean" page from Hanke's original copy—the basis for this edition—is presented and then followed by three correlative positive pages in the facsimile illustrations that can be viewed in the Critical Commentary online. As will be observed, the revisions to the Hanke positives are irreconcilable from one to the next, and thus they could not be used for informing this edition—or any edition, undoubtedly—except for possible corrections to Hanke's original work, and then for any unambiguous clarification of the original musical text. (A fully engraved, diplomatic transcription edition of the Hanke positives would serve future students of the "Emerson" material, and that task is left to the bravery of future musicologists.)

The Viola Part

The ending of Transcription 4 contains a line marked "Viola part (ad lib) *pp*—if played—but bringing out accent." Because there is an extensive, optional flute solo in the final "Thoreau" movement of the complete *"Concord" Sonata*, it would seem that this is an indication for a similar instrumental solo, however brief by comparison. This has led to debate that may be argued in either of two ways.

Those denying that this is an optional line for a viola would point to its correlative appearance in the extant *Emerson Overture* manuscript, in which it is assigned to the viola section and the first bassoon, with the initial note of each triplet also struck by a bell. In the evolution of the manuscript sources, Ives first adds this to the Reis copy as offset notes that would correspond to the bell part, then provides instructions to substitute either "Viola (or Bassoon part [in] score)," thus referencing the *Emerson Overture*. This would lend credence to an argument denying the optional performance of this line by a viola.

Arguing on the other side of the fence, supporters would indicate that all of the music in the *Transcriptions* was originally in the *Emerson Overture*—not simply the "Viola" line in question nor the other optional notes found in other sections of the piece—and yet no other material in the *Transcriptions* is identified in this way. A chief counter-example supporting this argument would be the overlapping chords in mm. 19–23 of Transcription 2, described above: provided their exact relationship to the *Overture*, why would Ives not annotate them as "Violins and Violas" to indicate their provenance? It would therefore seem odd that Ives would allow the melody to be labeled explicitly as "Viola part" (and ultimately published that way) unless he imagined the possibility of a performance by the stated instrument.

The decision as to whether the melody is to be played by an assisting violist (or at all, as it is an optional melodic line playable by the pianist) is therefore left in the lap of the interpreter, with both arguments as presented here for consideration.

Final Thoughts for the Analyst and Performer

From an analytical standpoint, a complete understanding of the "Emerson" music requires comparison of the following works by Ives: the "Emerson" movement in the 1921 printing and 1947 edition of the *"Concord" Sonata*; *Four Transcriptions from "Emerson"*; *Studies No. 1, 2, 9* ("The Anti-Abolitionist Riots in the 1830s and 1840s"), a piano solo based on the "centrifugal cadenzas" of the *Emerson Overture*; and *Study No. [11]*, based on the expanded ending of Transcription 4 as found in source Pc (as described in the Critical Commentary online). Braver souls still may wish to dive into the thorny brambles of the Hanke Positives, and great value would come from an examination of David G. Porter's reconstruction of the *Emerson Overture* and his related writings on it.

From a technical standpoint, Ives desired a performance of any version of the "Emerson" material to sacrifice tempo and rhythm in order to play the "right notes" in difficult passages. This stands in contrast to a performance of the "Hawthorne" material, where Ives felt that individual notes could be omitted or substituted with other notes in order to maintain a quick tempo where the music is tricky to execute.

From an interpretative standpoint, the performer might profit to consider the following, handwritten by Ives on a copy of the 1921 edition of *Concord*:

> This movement ["Emerson"] attempts to suggest the struggle that seemed
> to go on in Emerson, in reconciling the influence of the old Puritan canon,
> dogma, etc., with his individual growth—that is, theology vs religion. In fact
> the whole movement has more to do (and more than I intended) with the
> struggles of his soul than [with] that peace of mind which he commands
> even in his struggles—though the music tries to end with that feeling.

Thomas M. Brodhead

THREE-PAGE SONATA

Charles E. Ives
S. 89
Edited by
James B. Sinclair

rit.   Adagio

8va bass[a] [through m. 31?]

4

31   rit.

                                                    pp

35 Allegro

    ff

    [3]

octs [above?] -

40

44

49

53

[octaves continue through m. 58,2.♩?]

THE CELESTIAL RAILROAD
"Phantasy" for Solo Piano

Charles E. Ives
S. 116

Edited By
Thomas M. Brodhead
rev. ed. 2016

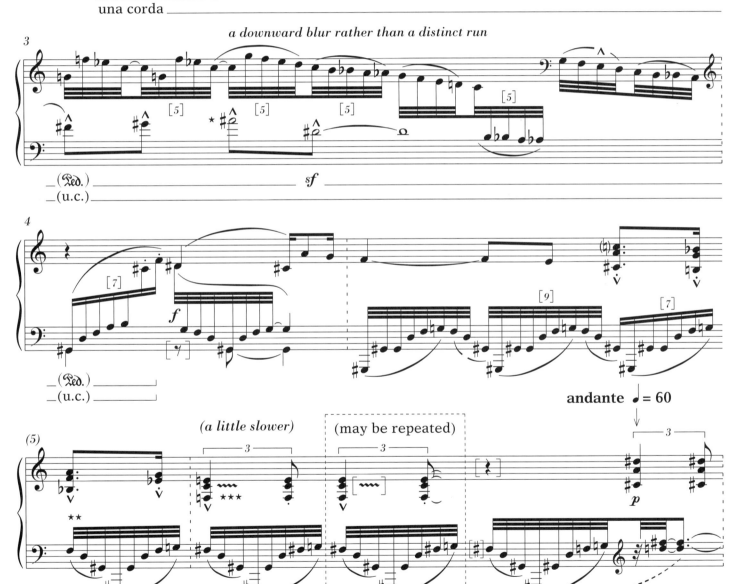

[NB: All footnote commentary is in Ives's own words except editorial commentary, which is in brackets.]

* [M. 3: The beamed half notes and the whole note are simply *l.v.* ♪s and ♩, respectively.]

** [M. 5:] (L.H. just a roll, not necessarily in exact time)

*** [M. 6:] On the middle C♮ I roll [i.e., trill] a B♮

8

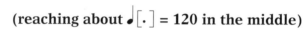

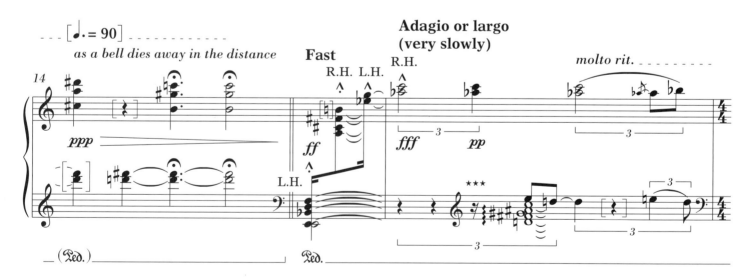

★ [M. 10: Throughout the score, slurs and ties with gaps are editorial; see Critical Commentary.]

★★ [M. 13:] may be prolonged if very fast—less abrupt [i.e., perhaps repeat the pattern a few more times if the maximum tempo of the *accelerando* is very fast.]

★★★ [M. 16: L.H. chord starting just after R.H.]

★ [M. 17: Play whole-note chord first, then grab B with left hand.]

★★ [M. 17:] just depress keys [of entire arpeggio] without striking as one chord [i.e., arpeggiate notes in random order.]

★★★ [M. 20: Top staff strikes a little after lower chords; follow horizontal sequence of notes and chords.]

★★★★ [M. 21:] Better to wait until lower chords die away a little before play[ing this] left-hand chord.

★★★★★ [M. 22:] The R.H. begins the 5/8 as the L.H. [sopra] ends the tune *ppp* .

★★★★★★ [M. 22:] (perhaps start this 8va lower [—] both hands [—] & go up [to *loco*] in 4th meas. [m. 25.]

* [M. 28:] these blows with the thumb should stand out—strike & leave [i.e., play all *sf* dyads as short eighth notes, even when tied to other notes, mm. 28–32.]

** [M. 29:] (LH through [m. 36] short hard blows)

*** [M. 31: Even though it's awkward,] if the LH strikes e♯ [then] the RH f♯ accent keeps strong

**** [M. 35: L.H. take G from R.H. —ed.]

***** [M. 36: The accelerando begun in m. 32 should continue proportionately here, with the note values halved in notation only.]

* [M. 37: Optionally alternate between *staccato* and *legato* in R.H. here through m. 40.]

** [M. 41:] I usually repeat here playing C♮ (for B♭) on repeat of 1st chord—keeping R.H. going in some

⌐5's [realized here, mm. 42–43.]

★ [M. 46: As with m. 41,] also repeat here making an extra $\frac{3}{8}$

★★ [M. 46: Sustain R.H. chord over L.H. pattern if boxed section is omitted.]

★★★ [M. 50: Play these chords with] sharp stroke[s,] as a bell [;] B♮ may be added with Thumb

a little faster
(not heavily, but accents strong)

★ [M. 62: See Critical Commentary on the possible use of an extra player here, mm. 62–76.]

★★ [M. 64:] L.H. accents very important here

★★★ [M. 67: L.H.] octs. [in parentheses] may be struck on accent[s] unless very fast

(quite fast) ♩ = about 152–160

★ [M. 85:] R.H. strikes a little behind L.H. as if written  etc. [through m. 87, 1st beat; perhaps only on main quarter beats: see arrowed lines.]

★★ [M. 87:] It may be better to hold this another beat — if so, tremolo it & play E♮ for D♮ at bottoms.

★ [M. 96: Broken slurs here and elsewhere are editorial; see Critical Commentary.]

★★ [M. 96: R.H. takes E *ad lib.*]

★ [M. 107:] paw these [dyads.]

★ ⌈M. 119:⌉ sometimes I omit this ⌈c♯.⌉

★★ ⌈M. 124: Ives wrote two different simultaneous slur phrasings for this passage in the MS; the pianist is free to interpret *ad lib.*⌉

stop with a jerk **very fast**

Allegretto ♩ = about 120 or slower
(a little slower)

These two measures [m. 135–136]
are more $\frac{2}{4}$ with a hold back on
last beat [rather than simply $\frac{5}{8}$
and $\frac{9}{16}$]

★ [M. 133:] I think the 2 rhythms are brought out better here if taken rather evenly & L.H. staccato but a
little louder than RH [Ives apparently is suggesting all notes in the L.H. to be played staccato and the
L.H. to be played slightly louder than the R.H.]

★★ [M. 134:] See next footnote.

★★★ [M. 135:] This bass really belongs to the upper time & if fast may be omitted or played *8va* [Ives draws
an arrow from this dyad to the location beneath the B+D♯+G♮ chord that precedes it in the previous measure, here with the dyad editorially indicated in brackets at the end of m. 134. That B+D♯+G♮ chord could
therefore be grabbed with the R.H. while the L.H. plays the F+C dyad, or following Ives's instructions, the
F+C dyad could be omitted.]

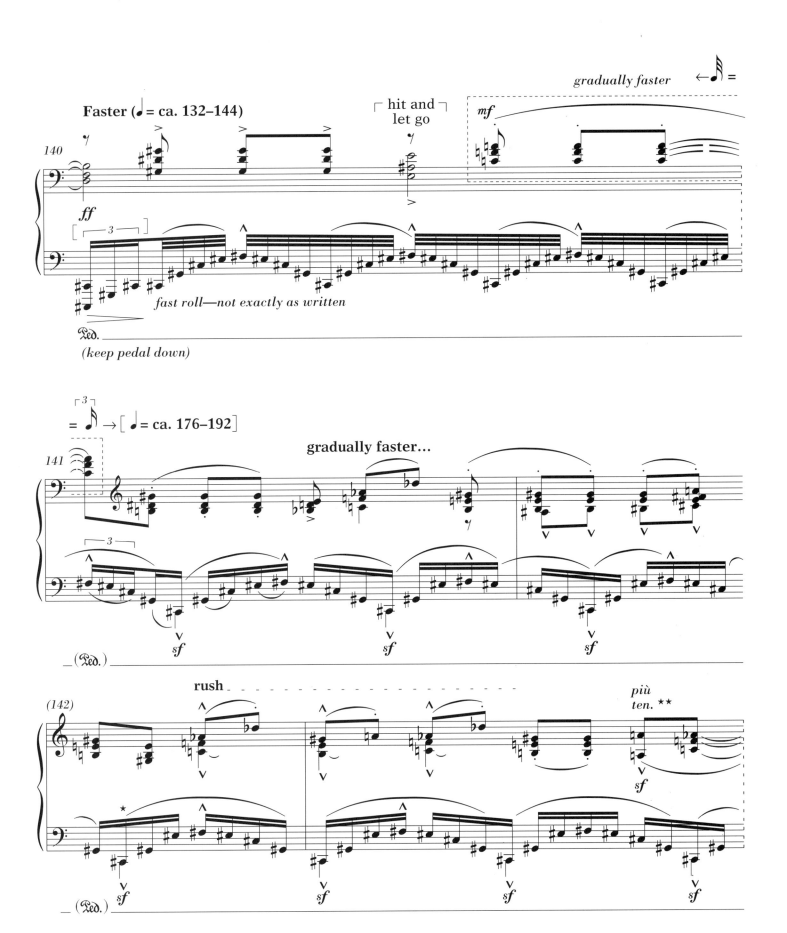

★ [M. 142:] (accent [the C♯s] so that the 7's [i.e., the pattern of 7 sixteenth notes] may be brought out)

★★ [M. 143:] hold a bit

(hold back a little)

con fuoco
(as fast as playable)

Largo (very slowly)
♪ = about 60

★ [M. 148:] pedal holds until after RH chord is struck [It's unclear whether Ives wants the pedal to extend to the G♮, as indicated notationally, or to end precisely where the G-major chord is struck in the R.H. The player may therefore decide which sounds better and interpret accordingly.]

Presto con furo—very fast again

[just a quick roll—not in exact time]

[m. 153–156 may be omitted]

as fast as playable

[may omit]

[L.H. plays upstemmed notes]

[R.H. plays downstemmed notes]

★ [M. 149: Ives apparently wants the D-major chord to sustain through this measure and also for it to be restruck as indicated; use of the sustain pedal would be the only tenable solution. See Ives's commentary in footnote ★★★★ for m. 161.]

★★ [M. 152:] I usually run this up through another octave [realized here as m. 153; see Critical Commentary.]

★★★ [M. 154–157: Strike the L.H. chords where they occur graphically, i.e., just after the final dyad of each quintuplet, almost as a grace-note chord to each subsequent quintuplet.]

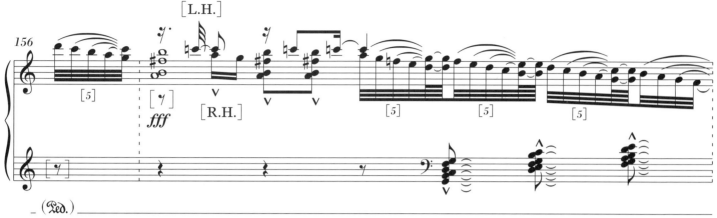

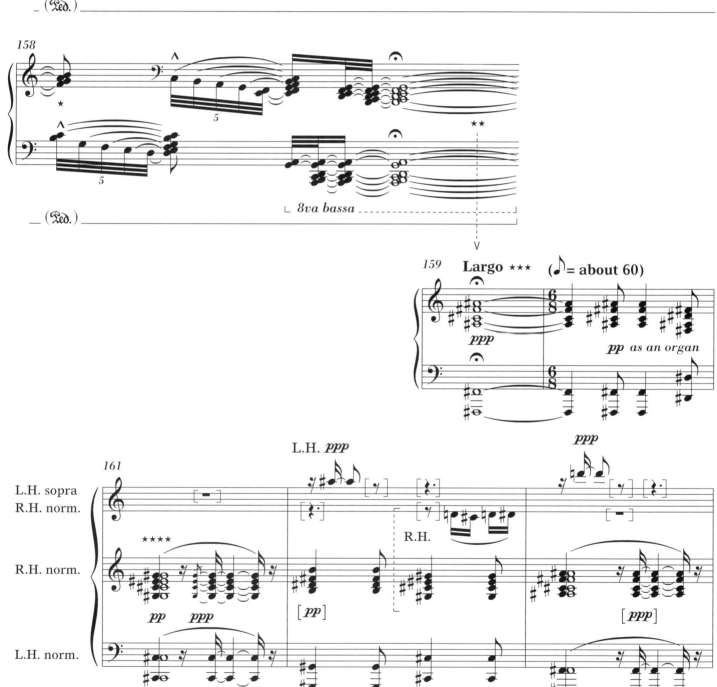

★ [M. 158:] (play so that all white notes will be sounding when F♯ chord (*pp*) [m. 159] is struck)

★★ [M. 158:] (not heard when struck—only after pedal stops.)

★★★ [M. 159:] (this chord & tune is [sic] supposed to emerge like an organ)

★★★★ [M. 161:] 1st chord is held by pedal through meas[ure]. [See footnote to m. 149 for clarification; likewise for m. 163 & 165.]

★ [M. 165: These L.H. notes] may be omitted

★★ [M. 169:] I hit this [chord] with [a] hard stiff arm

★ [M. 175:] Drawing up a little on this makes [the] passage easier

or

Original:

* [M. 181:] (lower E♮s may be omitted)

perhaps a little slower here

♩ = about 126–132

★ [M. 187–188: Ives indicates that the E octaves may perhaps be played 8ba lower.]

★★ [M. 190: These downstemmed notes in the R.H. are] not essential

roll [and] strike top E♮ [of second half-note chord] a little before beat ★

←♩ = ♩.→

♩. = about 138–144

(drum corps)

L.H. starts roll after R.H.

★ ⌈ M. 191: Ives apparently is suggesting a roll and grace note such as this:

★★ [M. 197: possibly double the upper L.H. notes with their lower octaves, here in parentheses, through m. 199.]

★★★ [M. 197: Tied staccato G♯ octaves in the L.H. are simply to be released *on* the beat where they occur, rather than to be re-articulated.]

very short and hard

(Bass Drum)   *sf*   *sf*

L.H. octave
lower ad lib.

perhaps a little slower and in a grandiloquent way

★ [M. 206:] omit [parenthetical g] if very fast

★★ [M. 209:] this B♮ sounds for a moment after the others [i.e., the other notes] stop [sounding.]

MUSIC APPENDIX I
The original opening in Ives's manuscript.

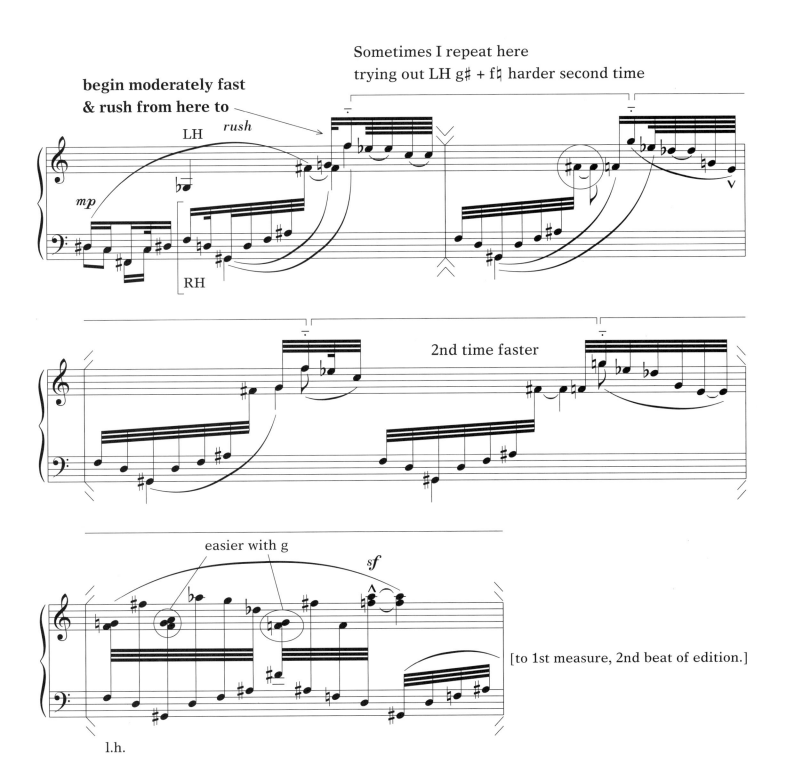

MUSIC APPENDIX II
The original opening in the Price Copy.

from here to next page as fast as playable. but lightly (—both pedals)

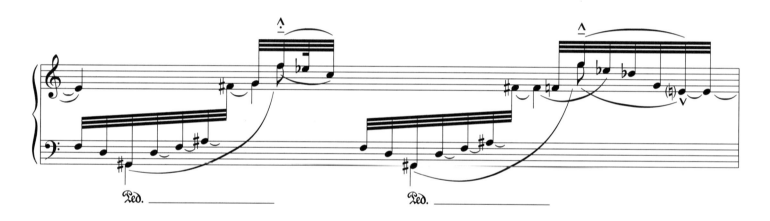

[to 1st measure, 2nd beat of edition.]

[INVENTION IN D]

Charles E. Ives
S. 118
Edited by
Geoffrey Block

MINUETTO, Op. 4

Charles E. Ives
S. 119
Edited by
James B. Sinclair

TRIO
Fine [14a]

D.C. al 𝄐

[false start, upside down at bottom of page]

SET OF FIVE TAKE-OFFS
The Seen and Unseen?
Sweet and Tough

Charles E. Ives
S. 122i
Edited by
James B. Sinclair

Rough & Ready et al.
and/or The Jumping Frog

Charles E. Ives
S. 122ii
Edited by
James B. Sinclair

Moderato (as Allegro as possible)

Song without (Good) Words

or The Good & the Bad (new & old)—
a little of both

Charles E. Ives

S. 122iii

Edited by
James B. Sinclair

Cantabile adagio

Scene Episode

Charles E. Ives
S. 122iv
Edited by
James B. Sinclair

Bad Resolution & Good WAN!

Charles E. Ives
S. 122v
Edited by
James B. Sinclair

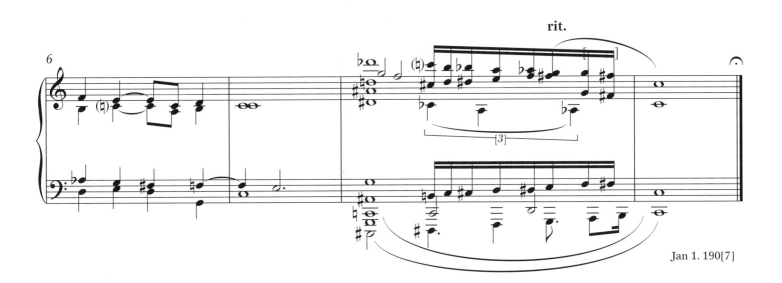

Jan 1. 190[7]

FOUR TRANSCRIPTIONS FROM "EMERSON"

Piano Solo

Charles E. Ives

S. 123
Edited By
Thomas M. Brodhead
rev. ed. 2016

* L.H. as a kind of declamation through here until [m. 14] but not enough so, to throw right hand out of a rather even sway.

*[L.H. on downstemmed notes]

★ D♮ & B♮ struck together but just after C♯.

★★ C♯ only *ppp* .

* Sometimes I...repeat [this phrase] with rit. [Ives]

* Omit E♮ *ad lib.*, unless E♮ & G can be struck together.

* Notes in ⌈curved⌉ brackets may be left out if very fast.

** ⌈D♯⌉ Just after L.H.

60

Slower [—] Maestoso

Moderately and easily

Hold Pedal!

Slowly

L.H. [upstemmed notes]

★ Sometimes better: F# C# G#

★★ [C♭] really a ¼ tone.

* Viola part (*ad lib*) **pp** —if played—but *bringing out accent.* [See front matter for commentary.]
** To be heard as a kind of overtone. *** Scarcely audible.

VARIED AIR AND VARIATIONS

Study No. 2 for Ears
or aural and mental exercise!!!

Charles E. Ives
S. 124
Edited by
James B. Sinclair

First protest, for "box belles" when "man" comes on stage

Allegro moderato or Andante con spirito

Allegro moderato
or Andante con spirito

64 [March time or faster]

Protest

Largo

pp

Adagio or Allegro

Applause (non-protest)

ffffffffffff

(con expressione)

Presto or so! Faster than ever or possible!

ffff

Allegro moderato
or Andante con spirito

WALTZ-RONDO

Charles E. Ives
S.125
Edited by
James B. Sinclair

Main Theme or Prin. Subj.

END
MAIN theme

Coda

Allegro vivace (or at least much faster than beginning)

THE "ST. GAUDENS"

("Black March")

Charles E. Ives
S. 683i
Edited by
James B. Sinclair

NEW YEAR'S DANCE

[Diplomatic Facsimile]

Charles E. Ives
S. 120
Edited by
James B. Sinclair

[PIECE IN G MINOR]
[Diplomatic Facsimile]

Charles E. Ives
S. 121
Edited by
James B. Sinclair